METRIC

THE MODERN WAY
TO MEASURE

METRIC

by Miriam Schlein

THE MODERN WAY TO MEASURE

Illustrated by Jan Pyk

HARCOURT BRACE JOVANOVICH
New York and London

The text of this book has been checked by a staff member of the National Bureau of Standards.

Text copyright © 1975 by Miriam Schlein
Illustrations copyright © 1975 by Jan Pyk

Printed in the United States of America

First edition

B C D E F G H I J K

Library of Congress Cataloging in Publication Data

Schlein, Miriam.
    Metric—the modern way to measure.

    SUMMARY: An introduction to the metric system, a
system of measurement which began in France approximately
two hundred years ago.
    1. Metric system—Juvenile literature. 2. Weights
and measures—United States—Juvenile literature.
[1. Metric system.   2. Weights and measures.
3. Measuring]   I. Pyk, Jan, 1934-   ill.   II. Title.
QC6.S34   389'.152   74-22169
ISBN 0-15-253187-4

Contents

What Is Measurement?

How do you find out how big something is?
You measure it—with a ruler or a tape measure.
And you find out it is so many *inches,* or so many *feet,*
or so many *yards* long. Or if you are riding a bike or
driving in a car, it is so many *miles.*

How tall is this baby giraffe, born in a zoo in the United States?

They measure him. He is 6 feet, 8 inches tall.

But suppose the same giraffe had been born in a zoo in France or Italy or Japan or in almost any other country?

They would measure him. And they would say he is 2 meters and 3 centimeters tall.

He is the same giraffe.

He is the same size.

But his size is described differently. The numbers and names are different.

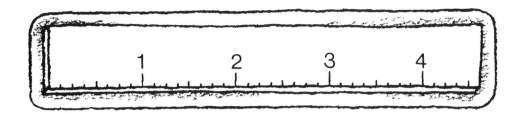

Why is this?

It is because we use a different system of measurement from the one they use in France and Italy and Japan and most other countries. Measurement in the United States is based on the *British Imperial System* of measurement. We use inches, feet, and yards. Most other countries use the *International Metric System* of measurement. They use millimeters, centimeters, and meters.

What is an *inch*, a *foot*, a *yard*?

What is a *millimeter*, a *centimeter*, a *meter*?

They are all units of measurement.

What is measurement?

Measurement is a way to describe the size of something. How long. Or how wide.

No matter what system you use, it is useful to be able to make an exact measurement so that you can describe the size of something—even if you do not have to measure a giraffe!

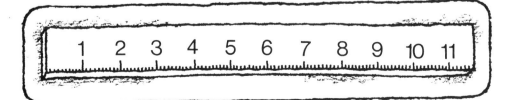

If you are building something, you can go to the lumberyard and say, "I need a piece of wood 31½ inches long." And the man can measure and cut a piece of wood for you exactly the right size.

If you were French, you would say, "I need a piece of wood 80 centimeters long." And the man would cut it just the right size.

The 31½-inch piece of wood is just about the same size as the 80-centimeter piece of wood. It is just described differently.

Using centimeters is a newer way of measuring. It began to be used only about two hundred years ago, in France.

Using inches is a very old way of measuring. People measured in inches thousands of years ago in ancient Rome.

2

Measurement Long Ago

Measuring something may seem like one of the most impersonal, mechanical things you can do. You take a ruler or a tape measure and lay it down, and you look at the numbers. You see that the box is 9½ inches long or your desk is 5 feet long.

But long ago, when people measured something, it was very personal. They did not use a ruler or tape measure the way we do. They used parts of their own bodies as rulers.

A man would use his hand, his fingers, his arm, his foot, to measure the size of things.

That is where our measure of a "foot" comes from. Thousands of years ago, the Romans, the Greeks, the Hebrews, the Egyptians all used their feet to measure with. A man could say, "This piece of cloth is 11 feet long." Of course it was not really exact because one man's foot is not exactly the same size as another man's foot. But it was a convenient and approximate way to describe size. And you would know, more or less, how much cloth he was talking about.

You can measure a man's foot—your dad's or your uncle's or your friend's. It is very close to 1 foot long. After a while, these ancient "feet" were standardized to be an exact measurement. The old Roman "foot" was 11.64 of our inches—a bit shorter than our foot. The old Greek "foot" was just a trifle longer than our foot.

Here are some Egyptians who lived about 5,000 years ago. They are using their arms to measure. They are measuring by *cubits*.

The cubit was the distance from a man's elbow to the tip of his middle finger.

The cubit* was an important unit of measurement in ancient times. The Greeks and the Hebrews and the Romans used it too.

The standard cubits varied from country to country. They were all close to about 20 of our inches.

*The word "cubit" comes from the Latin "cubitum," which means elbow.

Here is an ancient Greek. He is measuring something by using the *lick*. A lick was the distance from the tip of his thumb to the tip of his index finger.

Here is an ancient Hebrew. He is using a *span*. A span was the hand stretched out, from the tip of the thumb to the tip of the pinkie.

So the basis of measurement was the human body—the size of its parts or their relationship to one another.

There was another kind of measurement used that was based not on the size of the body but on its capacity to do a certain thing.

An *acre* used to be figured as the amount of land that could be plowed in one day by one man using one yoke of oxen. (It was not until the 1600's that the acre was standardized as 43,560 square feet. That's what it is now.)

One acre
43,560 square feet

A *talent* was a measure of weight used by the ancient Hebrews. A talent was the load that could be comfortably carried by a man. It came to about 58 pounds.

Even now, the height of a horse is still described in terms of "hands." People no longer literally use their hands to make this measurement. They use a tape measure. But if a horse is 60 inches high from the withers to the ground, they would say he is "15 hands." The hand has now been standardized to mean a measure of 4 inches. But the word "hand" is still used.

3

More Recent Measurement

The *inch* and the *mile* are body measurements, too.

The inch was the width of a man's thumb. "Inch" comes from the Latin word "uncia." Uncia means "twelfth part," because there were 12 uncia in one foot.

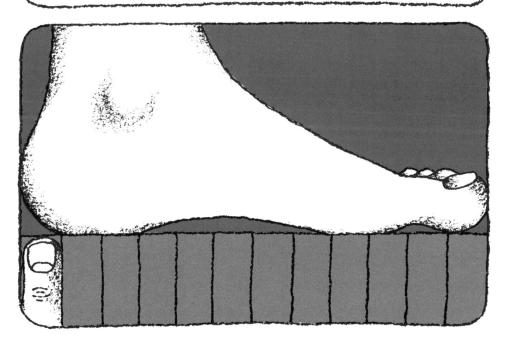

The *mile* was originally 1,000 paces of a Roman soldier. (A pace was two steps, which came to about 5 feet.) So, the Roman mile was 5,000 feet.

"Mile" comes from "mille," which means 1,000 in Latin, the language of the ancient Romans.

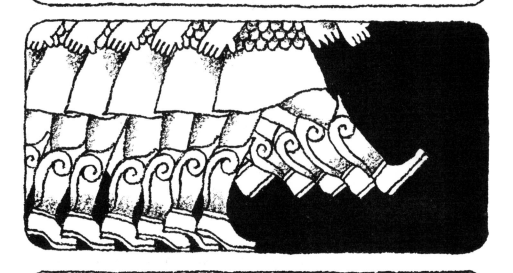

We don't use a span or a talent or a lick now. But we do use the inch and the mile in the United States. Why?

Because the inch and the mile were Roman measurements.

When the Romans invaded Britain more than 2,000 years ago in 55 B.C., they brought with them their system of measurement, which began to be used in Britain.

The "uncia," when it was adapted into the Anglo-Saxon language, began to be pronounced as "ynce," and later on "inch."

Since the United States began as a British colony, we naturally used the same measurements that the English used, which were originally ancient Roman.

In the 1100's, the English added a new unit of measurement. They added the *yard*. The word "yard" comes from "gird," which is the distance around one's waist. The measurement of one yard was the length of the sash worn by a Saxon leader.

This was not a very accurate standard. One leader could wear a longer sash than another leader. So, the *yard* was officially established as the distance from King Henry I's nose to the end of his thumb (with his hand outstretched).

In 1324, King Edward II changed the standard for the inch. From then on, an inch was no longer to be considered equal to a thumb width, but equal to the length of 3 grains of barley laid end to end.

Up until the 1800's, the standards for the yard, the foot, and the inch were not very exact. In 1830 in the United States it was found that different customs-houses were using measurements that were not quite the same, so they were all given standard measures to use. They were then all the same. But in the United States and in Great Britain it was becoming obvious that a much more precise standard for measurement was needed. What they finally used, in Britain, was something called the "Troughton bar."

This was a brass bar, 82 inches long. It got its name because it was cast by smiths named Troughton and Sims. It had marks made on it one inch apart. The British Imperial yard was then to be based on the precise distance between the 27th and 63rd inch marks on the Troughton bar. It was specified that the measurement was to be made when the bar was at a temperature of 62 degrees Fahrenheit. This was so that the length of the standard yard would not be changed even slightly because of expansion in the heat or contraction in the cold.

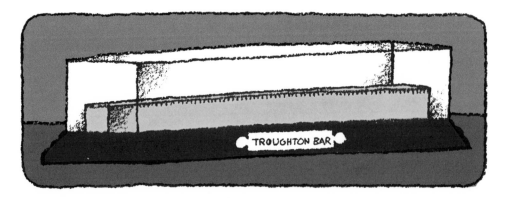

TROUGHTON BAR

For about fifty years, in the 1800's, the Troughton bar was used to determine the standard yard.

But at this time many other countries were beginning to use an altogether new system of measurement—one that they considered better than their old systems. It was called the METRIC SYSTEM. This system did not use anything like the old yard or foot or inch. It used a new main, basic unit called a *meter* (or *metre*).

In 1893, Britain and the United States decided they would no longer use the Troughton bar to define the yard. They would redefine the yard in terms of the meter.

Where Did the Metric System Come From?

What is a meter?

A meter is 39.37 inches long.

Why that size? Measured in inches, it seems a very odd size.

But the metric system has nothing to do with inches. The metric system of measurement is not based on the size of people's hands or feet. It is based on a physical fact of the earth. It is based on the distance from the North Pole to the Equator.

From the North Pole to the Equator is a distance of ten million meters. A meter is therefore one ten-millionth of the distance from the North Pole to the Equator.

Where did this idea come from?

In 1791, after the French Revolution, the French National Assembly met. They had many problems to face and changes to make in their country.

One of the problems was that measurement was not constant. People in one part of the country would measure things slightly differently from people in other parts of the country.

The French scientists had a solution to this particular problem. In a report to the French National Assembly, they advised that an entirely new system of measurement be used in France—one which they called the "metric system." (Meter means "measure" in Greek.) This new system was based on the dimensions of the earth rather than on the dimensions of man.

Scientists had been figuring out this system for some time before. Back in 1690, a Frenchman named Gabriel Mouton devised a system of measurement based on the length of a certain part of the great circle of the earth. This was the basis of what was later called the "metric system."

Scientists felt that after the French Revolution, when so many other changes were being made, was a good time to put this new system of measurement into common use.

What was so good about the metric system? Why was it better than the old ways of measuring?

First, the metric system was a "decimal system." This meant that the units of measurement—the meter, the centimeter, the millimeter, the kilometer, and so on—were all related to one another by 10's. And it is always easier to calculate by 10's. To multiply by 10, you just add a zero. Or, you can move the decimal point one place to the right. To divide by 10, you just move the decimal point one place to the left.

Second, if everyone were to begin to use this new system, the scientists said, it would solve the problem of having standards of measurements that varied slightly from one village to another. The standards of measurement would be exactly the same all over.

The scientists' recommendation was accepted. In 1799, the metric system was made the legal system of measurement in France.

There was one trouble. Most people simply did not use it. They kept on measuring in the old ways that they were used to. It was easier than learning a new way. For a while, Napoleon allowed people to use both systems. But in 1840, it was decided that there was only one way to get people to really switch from the old system to the new. That was to declare it against the law for anyone to use the old system of measurement. The metric system was made compulsory in France.

France was not the only country to start using the metric system. Other countries also began to adopt it because they felt it was a good system of measurement. Belgium, the Netherlands, and Luxembourg started in 1816; Italy, in 1845; Chile, in 1848; Greece, Cuba, and Puerto Rico, in 1849; Portugal, in 1852.

Between 1853 and 1863, nine of the Latin American countries began to use the metric system—Columbia, Panama, Ecuador, Venezuela, Brazil, Uruguay, Mexico, Argentina, and Peru.

One after another, countries all over the world converted to the metric system—Siam, Finland, Denmark, the Congo, Russia, and others. In 1951, Japan went onto the metric system.

Finally, just the English-speaking countries —England, Australia, Canada, and the United States—and a few small nations were the only ones left who were not using the metric system.

But in the 1960's, the British decided that it would be best if they, too, changed to the metric system.

Their entire economy started moving toward "metrication." Factories began converting their machinery—some slowly, some all at once—so that their products would be in sizes and measurements easily expressed in metric terms.

Milk, for example, would no longer come in quart bottles but in liter bottles. A single mattress is

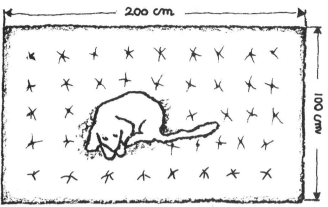

now made so that it is 100 centimeters by 200 centimeters, instead of a size expressed in feet and inches.

During this period, in the schools, young children were taught the metric system from the start. Others—the older children and the grownups—who had originally learned the British Imperial System, were still using inches and feet, but trying to become accustomed to figuring in millimeters, centimeters, and meters.

The year 1975 was the time set for the changeover to be completed, making Britain also a metric nation.

Along with Britain, Australia and Canada also have begun to change to the metric system. In fact, during the early 1970's there remained only five countries in the world who were not then or soon planned to be on the metric system. These were: Burma, Liberia, Muscat and Oman, Southern Yemen, and the United States.

Look at this map. Every country in the world, except those in white, are either now using the metric system or have decided by a certain time to switch over to it.

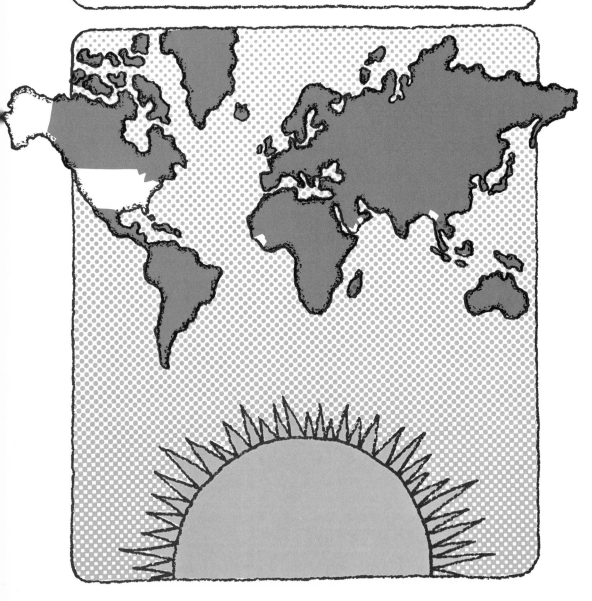

5

How Does the Metric System Work?

How does the metric system work? How does it compare with our system of inches, feet, and yards?

First, there is the *meter,* which is the basic size unit. A *meter* is equal to 39.37 inches. It is about 3½ inches longer than 1 yard.

Here are the units *smaller* than a meter:

Decimeter. There are 10 decimeters in 1 meter. A decimeter is 1/10th of a meter. So a decimeter is equal to 3.937 inches. It is a little less than 4 inches long.

Centimeter. There are 100 centimeters in 1 meter. A centimeter is 1/100th of a meter. So a centimeter is equal to 0.3937 of an inch. It is about 4/10ths of an inch or a little less than half an inch.

Millimeter. There are 1,000 millimeters in 1 meter. A millimeter is 1/1,000th of a meter, so a millimeter is equal to 0.03937 of an inch. This is about 4/100th or 1/25th of 1 inch.

Look at your ruler. Is each inch divided into eight little parts? Each of these little parts is about 3 millimeters long. A millimeter is very small.

The names of these units can help you remember their value. For these units smaller than the meter, the meaning comes from Latin.

"Deci" means one-tenth (1/10).

"Centi" means one-hundredth (1/100).

"Milli" means one-thousandth (1/1,000).

We have the related words "decimal" (system in tens), "cent" (one-hundredth of a dollar), "million" (one thousand thousand).

10 decimeters = 1 meter
100 centimeters = 1 meter
1,000 millimeters = 1 meter

You can see how these units are related by tens.

Let us compare the two systems very simply.

1 yard = 3 feet (36 inches)
1 foot = 12 inches
1 inch = 1/12th of a foot

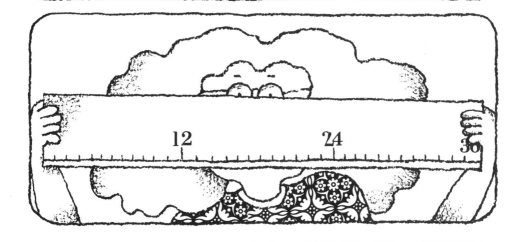

1 meter = 10 decimeters (100 centimeters)
1 decimeter = 10 centimeters
1 centimeter = 10 millimeters

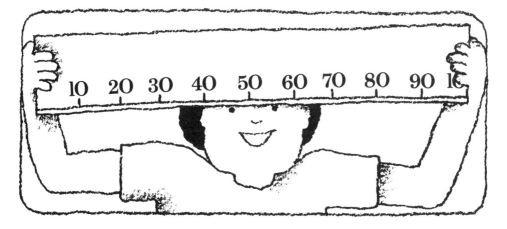

Suppose you want to figure how many inches there are in 17 yards. There are 36 inches in 1 yard. So, you would do this:

There are 612 inches in 17 yards.

Suppose you want to figure how many centimeters there are in 17 meters. There are 100 centimeters in 1 meter. So, you would do this:

$$\begin{array}{r} 17 \\ \times\ 100 \\ \hline 1700 \end{array}$$

There are 1,700 centimeters in 17 meters.

Which is easier? In which system would you be less likely to make a mistake?

Here are the units in the metric system *larger* than a meter:

Dekameter = 10 meters
Hectometer = 100 meters
Kilometer = 1,000 meters

The names for these larger units come from Greek.

"Deka" means 10.
"Hecto" means 100.
"Kilo" means 1,000.

Do you see how these are also related by tens?

10 meters = 1 dekameter
10 dekameters = 1 hectometer
10 hectometers = 1 kilometer

Travelers in Europe know about kilometers because the speed limits there are posted in kilometers per hour. The distances on the signs are also in kilometers.

A kilometer is about 6/10ths of a mile. (1 kilometer = 0.62 of a mile.) If the speedometer reads 100 (in kilometers), it means you are going just 62 miles an hour.

The metric system also has units to measure capacity, weight, area, and volume.

A *liter* (or *litre*) is the unit of capacity. It is used to measure amounts of liquid, like milk, and also materials like flour and sugar. A liter holds a little more than our liquid quart.

A *gram* is the unit of weight. It is about the weight of a paper clip.

A *kilogram* (which is 1,000 grams) is used to figure most weights. It is a little more than two pounds.

The *hectare* is a unit of area and is used to measure land. It is equal to a square measuring 100 meters on each side.

A *cubic meter* is the unit used to measure volume. It is a cube of which each edge is 1 meter.

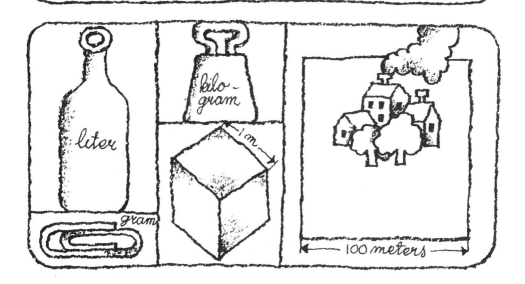

On page 60 at the end of the book, there is a table listing these units, and smaller and larger units.

On page 57 in the back of the book, there is a table listing U.S. units of measurement and telling you what they are approximately equal to in metric units. You might find it handy to refer to this sometimes. But if you really want to learn the metric system and be able to use it easily and comfortably, *do not try to memorize the facts in this table. Do not* say to yourself: "A foot is a little more than 30 centimeters," and try to remember that. If you do, you are still thinking primarily in feet and inches.

You must think of it the other way around. You must say to yourself: "A centimeter is a little less than a half inch." Or, "A meter is a little more than a yard; a liter is a little more than a quart." In that way, the metric unit will be the one that is significant in your mind and not the inch or the foot or the yard.

There is only one equivalency value you should memorize. It is this:

$$1 \text{ meter} = 39.37 \text{ inches}$$

The important thing you should keep in your head is the relationship between the different metric units themselves—that there are 100 centimeters in 1 meter, 1,000 millimeters in 1 meter, and so on. In that way, you will be "thinking metric." And soon you will no longer have to depend on inches, feet, and yards.

The Metric System and the United States

Have we ever considered using the metric system in the United States?

Yes, we have. For over 150 years, people have been arguing about whether or not we should go on the metric system. There have been Metric Societies formed that are *for* the metric system. One of these today is the United States Metric Association. There used to be Anti-Metric Societies that were strongly *against* the metric system, but none of these are in existence any more.

In 1821, John Quincy Adams, then Secretary of State, made a report to Congress dealing with weights and measures. The immediate problem our country had then was the lack of uniform standards. One way to solve this problem, Adams thought, would be for us to go on the metric system.

But most of our trade then was still with England, and it was therefore decided that it would be wiser for us to keep on using the same system of measures and weights used by the English. As a result, we did not go on the metric system. Later on, in the 1800's, Britain was considering going on the metric system but did not do so mainly because *we* were not using it! If the two nations had coordinated better with each other, perhaps we both would have been metric nations long ago. But that did not happen.

When Lincoln was president, the National Academy of Sciences was formed to advise the government on technical matters. In 1863, a committee of this group also recommended that the United States adopt the metric system. (By this time, many other countries were already using the metric system.) In 1886, Congress passed a law stating that it was permissible, but not compulsory, to use the metric system in this country.

In 1875, the International Bureau of Weights and Measures was formed in Sèvres, France. They constructed a new standard for the meter. Instead of using a platinum-end bar, which they had in the past, they redefined the meter in terms of a bar made of 90 percent platinum and 10 percent iridium, which was more constant and did not expand or contract so much.

They distributed copies of the new standard bar to countries that supported the bureau. We were one of these countries.

In 1890, President Benjamin Harrison received our standard meter bar, which was placed in our National Bureau of Standards in Washington. Now this bar is no longer the standard, either. In 1960, the meter was redefined as being 1,650,763.73 wavelengths of the orange-red light from the isotope Krypton-86, a rare gas. The advantage of this new standard is that it is even more precise, and it can be reproduced in any suitably equipped laboratory.

As far back as 1899, a bill was actually passed in the House of Representatives by a narrow margin of 119 to 117 stating that the metric system was to become the only legal system recognized in the United States. But great opposition arose at that time from anti-metric groups, and the bill was sent back to committee, where it died.

In 1893, the National Bureau of Standards did begin to use the metric system instead of the Troughton bar as the standard in legally defining the yard. The yard was to be defined in terms of the meter —that is, as 0.9144 of a meter. The foot was defined as 0.3048 of a meter. Officially, this made the United States a metric country in 1893.

But this really did not affect our everyday measurements, which were still made in inches, feet, and yards. We still talk about a 26-inch bicycle wheel or a room that is 15 by 25 feet. A girl still says she is 4 feet 5 inches tall.

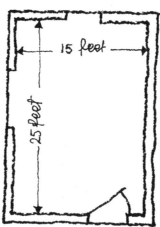

7

Why Go Metric?

Why have we held back so long from really becoming a metric country?

In the past, much of the opposition came from industry—from large manufacturers. They pointed out it would cost billions of dollars for American industry to change over to the metric system—for new machinery, for new tools that would fit the sizes determined by metric measurement, and for the time spent by their workers to get used to the new system.

But those who believe we should go on the metric system point out the following facts:

1. Most machinery now in use would *not* have to be discarded. It could be kept in use and adapted, by certain changes, to metric specifications.

2. Workers in all the other countries have been able to switch over from their traditional systems of measurement to the metric system. Why can American workers not do the same?

In fact, more and more people believe that it will be really harmful for American business if we continue to cling to our old system of measurement and do *not* change. They believe that American manufacturers will soon find themselves at a great disadvantage as the only non-metric large industrial nation in the world.

Our standards for steel bars, rods, tools, machines, and all parts will be different from the rest of the world's. Our sizes will not fit anyone else's. Measurement-wise, we are out of step.

Why is this important?

It leads to problems when we use machinery or equipment made in another country. We have difficulty in repairing it and in replacing parts be-

cause our tools, our nuts and bolts and pipes and rods, are all geared to a different scale of measurement. They don't fit.

And when we sell machinery or equipment to another country, they have the same problem in repairs and replacing parts. Because of this, other nations may more and more prefer to do business with metric-geared countries rather than the United States.

Here is a small example of the kind of problem you can have when the United States makes things to one standard of measurement and most other countries make their products according to another.

A boy wanted to fix a dining room table that was wobbly. He tried to tighten the bolts that held the legs to the top of the table. He tried his complete set of wrenches, but not one of them exactly fit the size of the bolts. He could not understand why. One of them should have fit.

Then he discovered what the problem was. The table was made in Denmark.

The bolts on the table were geared to metric measurement. The American-made wrenches were in sizes to fit American specifications.

Although the problem was solved finally by using a pliers instead of a wrench to fasten the bolts, a wrench would have done the job more easily and quickly.

This was a simple problem, but can you imagine how much more difficult it is when you are dealing with large, complicated machinery parts?

Now, standards for virtually everything made all over the world are in terms of metric measurment.

The metric system is now the "language of measurement" of the world.

Thus, many manufacturers here now no longer oppose it. They see the need for the change and are doing something about it. For example, General Motors and IBM are now converting their products to the metric system. Ford is also making some engines built to metric specifications.

In fact, in the United States, we have already been using the metric system in lots of ways. Your dentist uses it when he measures your teeth and makes mixes for fillings.

Your doctor and pharmacist use it when they figure amounts of medicine. Look at the prescription. It is in cc's (cubic centimeters) or in mg's (milligrams).

Boys and girls in school in the U.S. use it in many science classes.

U.S. scientists figure in the metric system, as do scientists all over the world. NASA scientists and engineers work in the metric system in their experimentation.

Distances in Olympic events are figured in meters. Every Olympic-size swimming pool used in this country either for practice or for competition is built to metric specifications. Our diving boards are at heights figured in meters: we have the 1-meter board (the low board), and the 3-meter board (the high board). This has been so for many years.

We use the metric system in still other ways:

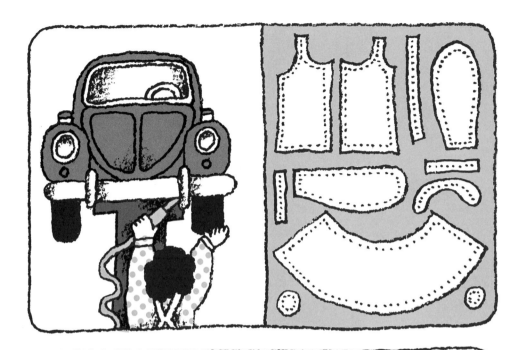

Your eyeglass lenses are ground according to metric tables.

The width of photographic film is expressed in millimeters.

It is the legal unit for electrical measure.

It is used by radio stations in defining the wavelength assigned to them

Auto mechanics have had to add metric tools to their equipment because there are so many foreign cars in this country today.

People who sew have noticed that clothing patterns now give fabric measurements in centimeters (cm) as well as in inches.

And so we almost seem to be switching into the metric system gradually and informally.

You may wonder why we, in the United States, cannot keep our own measurement system and still gear the sizes of things we make so that they will coordinate with objects made in metric countries. But this is not so easy.

The measurement system you use has a direct bearing on the way you select the dimensions and sizes of products. It is natural to select sizes that can be expressed as small whole numbers or simple fractions that are easy to remember and calculate within your own system of measurement.

Therefore, a metric-minded group, when setting the standards for, say, thin wire, might make it exactly 1 millimeter (equal to 0.03937 of an inch).

An inch-minded group would probably make it 0.04 of an inch.

This preference for using easy numbers in each of the systems has led to the incompatibility, for example, of steel bars and rods produced in the United States and those produced in metric countries. In the U.S., the sizes increase in jumps of 1/16th of an inch in small sizes, 1/8th of an inch in medium sizes, and 1/4th of an inch in larger sizes.

In metric countries, the sizes go up in jumps of 1, 2, or 5 millimeters.

It is natural to create sizes in terms of your own system of measurements. But you can see how it causes a problem. They are not interchangeable.

More and more people who have studied the matter believe it would be easier and better in the long run for the United States to convert to the metric system all at once, through a coordinated national program, instead of doing it bit by bit, as is happening now. This was the conclusion of those who took part in the U.S. Metric Study authorized by Congress in 1968. These were people representing industry, labor, transportation, education, real estate, law, science, and hundreds of other varied groups and professions in America.

Of course it would be confusing for a while for all of us who have figured in inches, feet, yards, and miles all our lives to suddenly start measuring things in centimeters and meters and kilometers. But it can

be learned. That has been shown by all the people in all the other countries who have already made the changeover. And it would be easy for young children learning it from the start, without having ever used the old system.

As was pointed out earlier, the metric system has already been adopted by almost every country in the world. When England and Canada and Australia have totally completed their changeovers, will the United States want to be the only large industrial

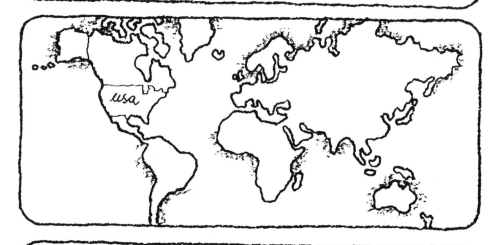

usa

nation not using the metric system? And yet, in the spring of 1974, by a vote of 240 to 153, the House of Representatives again voted against a bill that would "declare a national policy of converting to the metric system in the United States."

How long can we remain on the outside? It may not be practically possible for us to remain this way much longer. Perhaps by the time this book has been published, we may already be changing over to the metric system in our country. And some time in the future, perhaps the inch, the foot, the yard, and the mile will be units of measurement of the past—like the lick, the span, and the talent.

CUSTOMARY U.S. SYSTEM

Unit	Value	Metric Equivalent
Length		
Mile (mi)	5,280 feet	1.609 kilometers
(nautical mile)	6,080 feet	
Furlong (fur)	220 yards	201.168 meters
Rod (rd)	5.50 yards	5.029 meters
Fathom	6 feet	1.8288 meters
Yard (yd)	3 feet	0.914 meters
Foot (ft)	12 inches	30.480 centimeters
Inch (in)	0.083 feet	2.540 centimeters
Area		
Square mile (sq mi)	640 acres	2.590 square kilometers
Acre (a)	4,840 square yards	4,047 square meters
Square rod (sq rd)	30.25 square yards	25.293 square meters
Square yard (sq yd)	9 square feet	0.836 square meters
Square foot (sq ft)	144 square inches	0.093 square meters
Square inch (sq in)	0.007 square feet	6.451 square centimeters

(continued)

CUSTOMARY U.S. SYSTEM

Unit	Value	Metric Equivalent
Volume		
Cubic yard (cu yd)	27 cubic feet	0.765 cubic meters
Cubic foot (cu ft)	1,728 cubic inches	0.028 cubic meters
Cubic inch (cu in)	0.00058 cubic feet	16.387 cubic centimeters
Weight (Avoirdupois)		
Ton		
(short ton)	2,000 pounds	0.907 metric tons
(long ton)	2,240 pounds	1.016 metric tons
Hundredweight		
(short hundredweight)	100 pounds	45.359 kilograms
(long hundredweight)	112 pounds	50.802 kilograms
Pound (lb)	16 ounces	0.453 kilograms
Ounce (oz)	16 drams	28.349 grams
Dram (dr)	0.0625 ounces	1.771 grams
Grain (gr)	0.036 drams	0.0648 grams
Troy Weight (used for precious metals)		
Pound (lb t)	12 ounces	0.373 kilograms
Ounce (oz t)	8 drams or 20 pennyweights or 480 grains	31.103 grams
Pennyweight (dwt or pwt)	24 grains	1.555 grams
Grain (gr)	0.002083 ounces	0.0648 grams

(continued)

58

Unit	Value	Metric Equivalent
Apothecaries' Weight (used for medicines and drugs)		
Pound (lb ap)	12 ounces or 5,760 grains	0.373 kilograms
Ounce (oz ap)	8 drams or 480 grains	31.103 grams
Dram (dr ap)	3 scruples or 60 grains	3.887 grams
Scruple (s ap)	20 grains	1.295 grams
Grain (gr)	0.05 scruples	0.0648 grams
Capacity [U.S. Liquid Measure]		
Gallon (gal)	4 quarts	3.785 liters
Quart (qt)	2 pints	0.946 liters
Pint (pt)	4 gills	0.473 liters
Gill (gi)	4 fluidounces	118.291 milliliters
Fluidounce (fl oz)	8 fluidrams	29.573 milliliters
Minim (min)	1/60 fluidram	0.061610 milliliters
Capacity (U.S. Dry Measure)		
Bushel (bu)	4 pecks	35.238 liters
Peck (pk)	8 quarts	8.809 liters
Quart (qt)	2 pints	1.101 liters
Pint (pt)	½ quart	0.550 liters

METRIC SYSTEM

Unit	Value	Approximate U.S. Equivalent
Length		
Kilometer (km)	1,000 meters	0.62 miles
Hectometer (hm)	100 meters	109.36 yards
Dekameter (dam)	10 meters	32.81 feet
Meter (m)	1 meter	39.37 inches
Decimeter (dm)	0.1 meters	3.94 inches
Centimeter (cm)	0.01 meters	0.39 inches
Millimeter (mm)	0.001 meters	0.04 inches
Area		
Square kilometer (sq km or km²)	1,000,000 square meters	0.3861 square miles
Hectare (ha)	10,000 square meters	2.47 acres
Are (a)	100 square meters	119.60 square yards
Centare (ca)	1 square meter	10.76 square feet
Square centimeter (sq cm or cm²)	0.0001 square meters	0.155 square inches
Volume		
Decastere (dks)	10 cubic meters	13.10 cubic yards
Decistere (ds)	0.10 cubic meters	3.53 cubic feet
Cubic centimeter (cu cm or cm³/	0.000001 cubic meters	0.061 cubic inches

(continued)

Unit	Value	Approximate U.S. Equivalent	
		Dry	*Liquid*
Capacity			
Kiloliter (kl)	1,000 liters		
Hectoliter (hl)	100 liters	2.84 bushels	
Dekaliter (dal)	10 liters	1.14 pecks	2.64 gallons
Liter (l)	1 liter	0.908 quarts	1.057 quarts
Deciliter (dl)	0.10 liters	0.18 pints	0.21 pints
Centiliter (cl)	0.01 liters		0.338 fluidounces
Milliliter (ml)	0.001 liters		0.27 fluidrams
Mass and Weight			
Metric ton or tonne (MT or t)	1,000,000 grams	1.1 tons	
Quintal (q)	100,000 grams	220.46 pounds	
Kilogram (kg)	1,000 grams	2.2046 pounds	
Hectogram (hg)	100 grams	3.527 ounces	
Dekagram (dag)	10 grams	0.353 ounces	
Gram (g or gm)	1 gram	0.035 ounces	
Decigram (dg)	0.10 grams	1.543 grains	
Centigram (cg)	0.01 grams	0.154 grains	
Milligram (mg)	0.001 grams	0.015 grains	

Other Facts

The ordinary ton of 2,000 pounds is called a "short ton." In the United States, mining companies use the "long ton" of 2,240 pounds to weigh coal and iron ore.

Our "dry pint" (used to measure dry things —grain, fruit, etc.) is larger than our "liquid pint."

The U.S. pint = 16 ounces.

The English pint = 20 ounces.

The English gallon is 1/5th larger than the U.S. gallon.

The Imperial (English) gallon = 1 1/5th U.S. gallons.

The U.S. gallon = 231 cubic inches.

The English gallon = 277 cubic inches.

25

Centigrade

Celsius scale (also called the Centigrade scale) is used in metric countries. In this scale, water freezes at 0 degrees and boils at 100 degrees. This scale was devised by a Swedish astronomer named Anders Celsius in 1742.

25

Fahrenheit

Fahrenheit scale is used in the U.S. Water freezes at 32 degrees and boils at 212 degrees. This system was devised by a German physicist named Gabriel Fahrenheit in the 1700's.